Fables In Fog

Musings of a dreamweaver

Deepti Venugopal

BookLeaf
Publishing

India | USA | UK

Made with ❤ on the BookLeaf Publishing Platform
www.bookleafpub.in
www.bookleafpub.com

To my grandfather, who instilled a passion for storytelling in me and inspired me to aim for the skies. Thank you for nurturing my instincts to believe in the impossible.

My first book is dedicated to you.

Acknowledgement

I would like to express my deepest gratitude to my parents and grandparents for their unwavering support and encouragement. Your belief in my dream of writing a book has been my guiding light. Thank you for your endless patience, love, and wisdom, which have inspired me to pursue my passion. This journey would not have been possible without your constant support and faith in my abilities.

Preface

In the silent moments of our lives, we find our inner poet awakened. Through this collection of poems, I have attempted to capture multifarious emotions and musings and woven them through delicate threads of verse. Each poem is a reflection of the human spirit that experiences joy, anguish, passion, and contemplation.

As you turn these pages, you can find yourself on a journey of self-discovery. Some poems may resonate with your own experiences, while others may offer perspectives from the opposite lens. The beauty of poetry lies in the eyes of the beholder. Poetry is an expression that is subjective to everyone's reality.

Through this compilation, I invite you all to pause, reflect, and connect with the deeper currents of life. Whether you are a seasoned lover of poetry or a newcomer to its charms, I hope these poems will inspire, comfort, and provoke thoughts.

Thank you for embarking on this journey with me. May these poems be a source of solace and inspiration, and may they remind you that pen is always mightier than sword.

Ebony Masks and Purple hues

Color me intrigued, in purple hue,
Whispers of dusk, where truth's askew.

Shrouded in veil, where hypocrisy hides,
Masking in ebony, virtue slides.

Donning a robe, in regal guise,
Fake veneers conceal the lies.

Behind closed doors, schemes propel,
And echoes of deceit secretly dwell.

Mask of grace hides shades of green,
Engulfing the thorns with velvet sheen.

With every dawn, loyalties are betrayed,
And with truths, the trust is decayed.

Journey through the memory lane

Meandering through the memory lane,
I recall a life void of pain.
Where laughter was not an anomaly,
And all the kids were mostly jolly.

In the playground, we would run,
Beneath the heat of the scorching sun.
Where friendship bloomed in every nook,
And laughter echoed as we shook.

Forging bonds through stealthy notes,
Hiding secrets in concealed quotes.
Behind every story, a lesson learned,
Hearing echoes of dreams returned.

Simpler times are our cherished past,
Where still a world of innocence lasts.

A realm of wonder

Within the confines of human mind,
Resides a boon so divine.

A select few are blessed to mine,
A realm of innovation, to unwind.

Under the canvas of golden hue,
One imagines a sky not so blue.

A world that weaves and defies time,
Crafting a reality completely sublime.

Take a flight of faith-filled view,
And engulf your world with dreams anew.

With every sapling, a story grew,
Making your visions a dream come true.

Season of Change

Amidst nature's palette of crimson and gold,
A canvas emerges, mentioned in tales of old.

Fluttering leaves, break the silence,
Harbinger of nature's semblance with guidance.

Beneath the canopy, shadows play,
Wilderness whisper, bloom, and stay.

As I linger around, under the scorching sun,
My heart craves for some summer fun.

Eye of the storm

At the stroke of midnight,
When darkness claims its right,
An ember of hope ignites,
Overpowering the plight of fright.

Mind awakens to endless possibility,
Filled with dreams of alternate reality,
Forged with a different mentality.

Escaping the clutches of misery and gloom,
Embracing the vitality of bloom,
A heart stood firm in the eyes of the storm,
With the head held high, weathering the storm.

Breaking the shackles of norm,
To create a new form,
By leading the reform.

An Outcast

Amongst the crowd,
A spirit stood tall,
Not pretentious but self-assured.
Breaking the shackles of the thrall.

Defying the blend,
I choose to transcend.
My beacon being my self-belief,
Weathering the storm of grief.

Charting my course,
I find strength surging from my source.
By staying steadfast,
At the risk of being an outcast.

An enigma

I am the enigma to behold,
I am the secret that's untold.

I am the echo of the past,
Guarding the relics that forever last.

I am a future that remains unseen,
A mere dream in realms between.

I am the hope for an obscure night,
Resembling the spark that chases away your
fright.

I begin at the close,
Where the mystery timely disclose.

Grit and grind

With compass set and eyes ablaze,
An explorer ventures without a daze.

Every morn with relentless drive,
She seeks the truth to survive.

The thrills of trails that twist and bind,
She carves her path with grit and grind.

In whispers old of ancient lore,
She can't ignore the call to explore.

In every curve, she finds a quest,
A determined soul who doesn't rest.

Every night she survived,
Is a testament to what she contrived.

Scent of the wild

First fragrance of rain, scent of the wild,
Descent of calm, with drips pure and mild.

Carrying hints of wood with entwined roots,
Reviving spirit, with hopes of reboot.

Nature's symphony, with its divine charm,
Enamors the world with its soothing balm.

A luscious scent, we call petrichor,
An essence of rebirth that we adore.

Rustling leaves, harbinger of soothing sound,
Rejuvenates the world with freshness newfound.

Arching rainbow, with colors pristine,
Astonished the world of nature's design.

A wordsmith's craft

With quill in hand, a writer spins,
Tales of glory thus begin.

With spills of ink, ideas are framed,
With structured flow, chaos is tamed.

With captured dreams in silent night,
Sparks of passion take flight.

With every lore, history unfolds,
Masked as legends, the story is told.

Enraptured readers hold on tight,
Let your imagination soar with delight.

A wordsmith's craft is mesmerizing sight,
Weaving art that ignites

Moments of stillness

When the clock strikes twelve,
Our world stands still.

Pausing the moments for us to delve,
In the ebony sky, we seek some tranquil.

The night unfurls its downy cloak,
In flickering shadows, our dreams evoke.

When the clock strikes twelve, strive to reflect,
In fleeting moments, what not to neglect.

Seize the time to recoup and persevere,
To build a future that we revere.

In silence that's vast, our mind aligns,
To greet the morn, with innovation that shines.

Forgotten legacy

In a room untouched, from a decade ago,
Dust settles with a morning glow.

Hiding in plain sight lies a clue,
A symbol of legacy, obscure yet true.

With edges frayed, its colors fade
Capsules of the past, reminiscence cascade.

A portrait drawn with a sepia tone,
A relic of the past, artist unknown.

Captured moment unveils a tale,
In the forgotten room lies its trail.

A slice of antiquity, a family's pride,
In the tranquil stillness, secrets reside.

The Night mystique

Amidst the shadows of tranquil night,
A mysterious circus promises delight.

Air thickens with murmured lore,
Of the parallel world and tales of yore.

A jester's smirk, missed in fleeting glance,
An acrobat's soar engulfs you in trance.

With delectable sweets that taste divine,
A lure to your senses, a cunning design.

Ringmaster's eyes resemble snare,
A hidden trap, so tread with care.

Careful what you wish for, beware of grandeur,
Betrayal awaits behind closed doors.

Owning narrative

Own your story, own your narrative,
Not self-centered, just an assertive spirit.

Sharing joys, highs, and lows,
Not for applause, but to disclose.

Standing my ground, I speak my mind,
Not immature, not unrefined.

Chasing passion with unrestricted glee,
Not seeking approval, just being me.

When you psychoanalyze my vibrant side,
Know it's my essence, not foolish pride.

Still if you judge, just take a pause,
Know I am an original, with all my flaws.

Tales of champions

In tales and fables, both old and new,
One cheers for heroes, getting their due.

One discovers courage, faith, and might,
In stories told with astute foresight.

Potter with his rebellious streak,
Defied the power of dark and bleak.

With swords and bows and friends of old,
Pevensies bravery was foretold.

With power of seas and might do fierce,
Percy won all fights, facing his fears.

In realms of fantasy, where these heroes dwell,
Their deeds of valor cast a bewitching spell.

Wings of fire

When darkness rises and plagues the night,
Rebels rise with fiery might.

Against the tide, they find their stride,
With ambitious vision, their dreams abide.

Unreasonable norms are truly defied,
Challenging forms they valiantly ride.

Resembling a beacon, glimmering through
nights,
Claiming justice, they fight for their rights.

Giving voice to those who can't speak,
With courageous acts, they stand for the meek.

Like a Phoenix, from ashes they rise,
With ignited winds, they aim for the skies.

Silent stars

With tranquil minds, the shy ones tread,
Believing in actions, with words unsaid.

While the taciturn folks, with their intonation
low,
Articulate their thoughts, more than we know.

Bashful souls detest eyes that pry,
Tired of judgment, afraid to try.

While the taciturn folks bide their time,
To assert their views, with prose or rhyme.

In their defiant way, their convictions ignite,
Validating their worth with vigorous might.

Carving their destiny, as they are,
They brave the tempest, like a fiery star.

Through the looking glass

Resembling a future that's unknown,
A life built on fantasy is condoned.

In realms where dreams and hope expand,
A world exists called wonderland.

The white rabbit who is always late,
Is the personification of our hasty state.

Down the hole, with choices to make,
An adventure begins with life at stake.

One stumbles across a Cheshire cat,
with a grin askew,
Who guides your way in a maze,
where riddles of life ensue.

There is a mad hatter with his ceaseless tea,
Who shows you how a bit of chaos can set you
free.

Elemental harmony

Here's a story of elemental force,
Engulfed in nature's primal course.

Earth with its history old,
In every particle, a tale is told.

Rivers gushing with might and poise,
Holds life's secrets, beneath all noise.

From hearth to forge, fire burns with passionate
rage,
Enkindling path in every age.

Air, a breath of vitality,
Balms the heart with intense serenity.

Blended together, they sustain the soul,
Creating a symphony, uniting us whole.

Respite in solitude

In a world filled with monotonous grind,
A brief respite is hard to find.

In moments of serenity, vision is materialized,
In tranquility of solitude, dreams ignite.

To carve our milestone,
We hustle alone.

In Eden of our mind,
Vines of hope intertwine.

Balance life with utmost care,
Take a plunge with audacious dare.

No guilt should dampen your precious hour,
Avoid the people who are dour.

A treasure trove

In enclosed pages, fables unfold,
A treasure trove with tales of gold.

From archaic scrolls to contemporary prose,
Our views expand, and wisdom grows.

A world of wonder, thrills, and dreams,
Books are more than what they seem.

With every twist a new surprise,
Journey taken in disguise.

A writer's essence, a canvas vast,
Colored with ink, preserved to last.

In a fictional universe, we challenge our
thoughts,
Seeking fortune, battles are fought.